Knock! Knock!

Where Is There?

by Brian Elling

illustrated by Andrew Thomson, David Groff,
Kevin McVeigh, and Nancy Harrison

Penguin Workshop

PENGUIN WORKSHOP
An Imprint of Penguin Random House LLC, New York

Copyright © 2019 by Penguin Random House LLC. All rights reserved.
Published by Penguin Workshop, an imprint of Penguin Random House LLC, New York.
PENGUIN and PENGUIN WORKSHOP are trademarks of Penguin Books Ltd.
WHO HQ & Design is a registered trademark of Penguin Random House LLC.
Printed in the USA.

Visit us online at www.penguinrandomhouse.com.

Library of Congress Cataloging-in-Publication Data is available upon request.

ISBN 9781524792084   10 9 8 7 6 5 4 3 2 1

CONTENTS

Why are the steps to the <u>Parthenon</u> so slippery?
Because they're in *Greece*!

HYSTERICAL HISTORICAL PLACES

Knock! Knock!
Who's there?
I'm China.
I'm China who?
I'm *China* **see over this** Great Wall!

What did the Egyptian pharaoh want to put in his pyramid?
Everything but the kitchen *sphinx*!

What do you get when you cross the man who built the Tower of London and a sweet potato? Will-*yam* the Conqueror!

Knock! Knock!
Who's there?
Vespasian.
Vespasian who?
Ves-pas-ian through Rome and stopped at the Colosseum!

Why did the Greeks stop building the Parthenon?
So they wouldn't have to start calling it the *Whole*-thenon!

Knock! Knock!
Who's there?
Nixon.
Nixon who?
Nix-on the Great Wall of China **were caused by arrows!**

What did the king of the Incas say when he sneezed?
Achoo Picchu!

Knock! Knock!
Who's there?
Camel.
Camel who?
***Camel* the way from North America to see the pyramids!**

Why did the juice box take a vacation to Asia?
To see the *Grape* Wall of China!

Knock! Knock!
Who's there?
Vine.
Vine who?
Vine with me if you want to visit Machu Picchu!

Why are there so many gardeners at the Tower of London?
Because of all the *trees*-on!

What do you get when you cross the Colosseum and a muscle ache?
A *cramphitheater*!

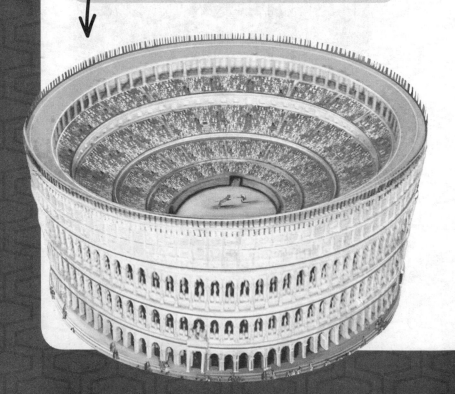

Knock! Knock!

Who's there?

Nero.

Nero who?

Ner-o far, you can see the Colosseum **from anywhere in Rome!**

What game did the mom play with her baby when they visited Peru? Machu *Picch-u-boo*!

Knock! Knock!

Who's there?

Athena.

Athena who?

Athen-a **Greek goddess at the** <u>Parthenon</u>!

Knock! Knock!

Who's there?

Terrace.

Terrace who?

***Terrace* a lot of mountains around** Machu Picchu!

What did the gladiator say after his last fight at the Colosseum?

I *sword* I'd never fight again!

Why did the pyramid cry when it got lost?

It wanted its *mummy*!

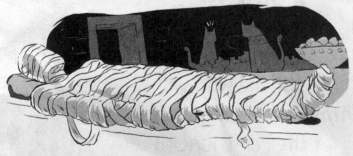

Why did the man with an ax do flips at the <u>Tower of London</u>? To prove he had great *execution*!

Knock! Knock!
Who's there?
Defense.
Defense who?
De-fense around China wasn't strong enough. So they built a wall!

What did the builder say when his pyramid fell down? "If at first you don't succeed, try, *triangle* again!"

Knock! Knock!
Who's there?
Soldier.
Soldier who?
Sold-ier **photos of the**
Great Wall of China!

Why did the warrior smile in the Colosseum?
Because he was a *glad*-iator!

What did King Tut say when he found out that his pyramid was so tiny?
"Hey, that's not *fair*-aoh!"

Why do ghosts like the
Tower of London?
Because the Crown Jewels are so *boo*-tiful!

Knock!
Knock!
Who's there?
Roy.
Roy who?
Roy-alty were
the only people
who lived at
Machu Picchu!

What do you get when you cross the <u>Great Wall of China</u> with an orca?

The Great *Whale* of China!

Knock! Knock!

Who's there?

A crown.

A crown who?

A-crown the year 1078, the Tower of London **was built!**

**Knock!
Knock!**
Who's there?
Zoo.
Zoo who?
Zoo you know that wild animals used
to live in the Tower of London?

What did the explorer say when
he fell on the pyramid?
"Now I get the *point*!"

Why did the gladiator feel
like the entire Colosseum
was watching him?
Because of all the *stairs*!

What do you get when you cross a carving of a horse at the Parthenon with a penny?
A *cent*-aur!

Why is there so much quacking at Machu Picchu?

Because of all the aque-*ducks*!

What do you get when you cross a gladiator in the Colosseum with a cow?

A *cattle* to the death!

Knock! Knock!
Who's there?
Archie.
Archie who?
Archie-tects designed the Great Wall of China!

What do you get when you cross a pyramid and some graph paper?
A pyra-*grid*!

Knock! Knock!

Who's there?

Apollo.

Apollo who?

A-*pollo* stone is all that remains of the Parthenon!

What did the Great Wall of China say when the music was too loud?

"You're hurting my engin-*ears*!"

Why is the letter *C* afraid of the Tower of London?

Because of all the *B*-headings!

What's the best way to travel to famous ruins in Peru?
On the Machu *Picchu-choo* train!

Knock! Knock!
Who's there?
Patrick.
Patrick who?
Pa-trick-ed me by hiding in a pyramid!

What did the emperor say when he ran out of bricks for the *Colosseum*?

Don't *quarry* about it!

Why does the Great Wall of China make people happy? Because it's more than four thousand *smiles* long!

Knock! Knock!
Who's there?
Cairo.
Cairo who?
Cai-ro, **row, row your boat all the way to the pyramids!**

Knock! Knock!
Who's there?
Hades.
Hades who?
Ha-des **marble steps lead to the Parthenon!**

Knock! Knock!
Who's there?
Alpaca.
Alpaca who?
Al-paca **your suitcase so we can go to** Machu Picchu!

Why do people in the Tower of London wear short sleeves?
Because they're in an *arm*-ory!

What did the magician say when he did his disappearing act in Rome?
Colosseum, now you don't!

Knock! Knock!
Who's there?
Machu.
Machu who?
Ma-chu-s her food like a llama!

How do you know the famous buildings in Egypt are old?
Because they're the Pyramids of *Geezer*!

Why did the man pet the lion in the Colosseum?
He was the em-*purr*-or!

What did the Great Wall of China say when a bulldozer tried to knock it down? "Hey, don't take me for *granite*!"

Knock! Knock!

Who's there?

Anne.

Anne who?

Anne-other day at the Tower of London!

Why did the architect of the Parthenon rub his head?

Because he had a pain in his *temple*!

What did Zeus say when a cannonball hit the Parthenon?

"Aw-crap-olis!"

Why did the **Colosseum** get a foot rub?

Because its *arches* hurt!

Knock! Knock!

Who's there?

Beth.

Beth who?

Beth you can't guess where the Tower of London is!

Who gives the Great Wall of China a haircut?
Barber-ians!

Why was the builder of the Parthenon late to work?
I don't know. Why don't you *column*?

Knock! Knock!
Who's there?
Allen.
Allen who?
Allen-t my hammer to a pyramid builder!

Knock! Knock!

Who's there?

Raven.

Raven who?

***Raven* about the** Tower of London **is easy!**

Knock! Knock!

Who's there?

Senator.

Senator who?

***Sen-a-tor* group to visit** the Colosseum!

NATURAL BLUNDERS

Knock! Knock!

Who's there?

Iguana.

Iguana who?

I-guana **go to the** Galapagos Islands!

Why is the Great Barrier Reef
so amazing?
Because it's in *Awe*-stralia!

**Knock!
Knock!**
Who's there?
Mist.
Mist who?
Mist **watching someone going
over** Niagara Falls **in a barrel!**

Knock! Knock!

Who's there?

Canoe.

Canoe who?

Canoe **tell me how to row through the** Grand Canyon?

What did the scientist say when her assistant said it was hot in Antarctica? "I'm not sure I *degree* with you!"

Why did the lazy climber never reach the top of Mount Everest?

Him-a-layan down too much!

Knock! Knock!
Who's there?
Anemone.
Anemone who?
An-emone **of the** Great
Barrier Reef **is pollution!**

Why is Niagara Falls always scared?
Because it's near Lake *Eeeeerrie*!

Which president loves
the Grand Canyon?
Gorge Washington!

What did the scientist say when she got stuck on an iceberg in Antarctica?
"Go with the *floe!*"

How long does it take to climb the tallest mountain in the world?
Foreverest!

Knock! Knock!

Who's there?

Whale.

Whale who?

***Whale*, I guess we have to migrate to the** Galapagos!

Why do corals in the Great Barrier Reef like to kiss?
Because they have so many pol-*lips*!

What do you get when you cross a storm in Antarctica and a reptile?
A *blizzard*!

What type of test does Niagara Falls like to take?
True or *falls*!

Knock! Knock!
Who's there?
Frigate.
Frigate who?
Frigate Hawaii! I want to visit the Galapagos!

Knock! Knock!
Who's there?
Mule.
Mule who?
Mule have to hike to the Grand Canyon.

What do you get when you cross the **Great Barrier Reef** and some silverware? A blue la-*spoon*!

Why did **Niagara Falls** have to sit on the bench during the basketball game? Because of all its water-*fouls*!

Knock! Knock!
Who's there?
Eva.
Eva who?
Eva-lanche on **Mount Everest!**

Why are the beds in Antarctica so cold?
Because of all the *ice* sheets!

Which seabird on the Galapagos has the most positive attitude?
The peli-*can*!

Why did the Grand Canyon put on pants?
So the tourist couldn't see its *buttes*!

Why is Niagara Falls so clean?

Because the *Maid of the Mist* is always cleaning it!

**Knock!
Knock!**
Who's there?
Hillary.
Hillary who?
Hillary-ous jokes about Everest
made the explorer laugh!

Who's the most famous dog in
the Great Barrier Reef?
Scuba-Dooby-Doo!

Why is it illegal to take seashells from the Galapagos?
Because you might interfere with natural *shell*-ection!

What do you get when you cross a snake from the Grand Canyon and a happy baby?
A *rattler*!

Knock! Knock!
Who's there?
Moss.
Moss who?
Moss **of the plants in** Antarctica **are very small!**

What do you get when you cross
Niagara Falls and a pizza?
Pie-agara Falls!

**Knock!
Knock!**
Who's there?
Albert.
Albert who?
Albert-tross live in the
Galapagos!

Why did the tallest
mountain in
the world stop
playing tennis?
It hurt its Ever-*wrist*!

**Knock!
Knock!**
Who's there?
Icy.
Icy who?
Icy **a lot of snow in** Antarctica!

Why doesn't the Grand
Canyon wear shoes?
So you can see its plat-*toes*!

**Knock!
Knock!**
Who's there?
Goby.
Goby who?
Goby **one with nature at
the** Great Barrier Reef!

What do you get when you cross some coral and a cow?

Great Barrier *Beef*!

Knock! Knock!

Who's there?

Wendy.

Wendy who?

Wen-dy **water freezes on** Niagara Falls, **you can walk to Canada!**

What did the monster say to her mom while climbing Mount Everest?

Are we there *yeti*?

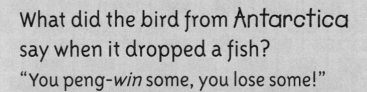

What did the bird from Antarctica say when it dropped a fish?

"You peng-*win* some, you lose some!"

Knock! Knock!

Who's there?

Cave.

Cave who?

Cave **you a map to the** Grand Canyon!

What did the guide say when his dad asked him to climb Everest?

Sher-pa!

What did the shrimp say when he got swallowed by a blue whale in Antarctica?

"Please don't *krill* me!"

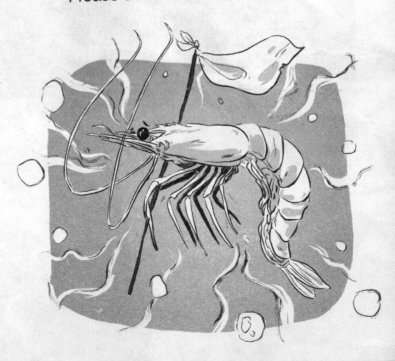

Knock! Knock!
Who's there?
Island.
Island who?
Island near the Great Barrier Reef **tomorrow!**

Knock! Knock!
Who's there?
Ken.
Ken who?
Ken someone turn off Niagara Falls?

What do you get when you cross the Grand Canyon and a coloring book? The Grand *Crayon*!

Why did the mountain climbers do math on their way up Everest? Because they had to *sum*-mit!

Knock! Knock!
Who's there?
Dugong.
Dugong who?
Du-gong too far if your ship hits the Great Barrier Reef!

Knock! Knock!
Who's there?
Goat.
Goat who?
Goat to the Galapagos to see some awesome animals!

What do you call it when your barrel doesn't make it over the waterfall?
A Niagara *Fail*!

What did the scientist say when her assistant said there was no ice in Antarctica?
"Are you gla-*sure* about that?"

Knock! Knock!
Who's there?
Al.
Al who?
***Al*-titude sickness will getcha on** <u>Everest</u>!

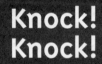

Knock! Knock!
Who's there?
Ives.
Ives who?
***Ives* been thinking about a trip to the** Grand Canyon.

What does the Great Barrier Reef
do when it wants to take a nap?
It goes *snore*-keling!

Why is it difficult to close your
Tupperware in Antarctica?
Because it's hard to get a good *seal*!

How do tiny birds hop around the
Galapagos Islands?
Finch by *finch*!

Knock! Knock!

Who's there?

Crab.

Crab who?

Crab **your bathing suit!
We're going to the**
Great Barrier Reef!

**Knock!
Knock!**
Who's there?
Yak.
Yak who?
Ya-kan **count on me to carry your equipment up** Everest**!**

What did the park ranger say when she saw litter in the Grand Canyon?
"Hey, who made a *mesa* in here?"

**Knock!
Knock!**
Who's there?
Evan.
Evan who?
Evan **I've been to** Niagara Falls**!**

What do you get when you cross a Mount Everest guide and a marker? A *Sherpie*!

What do you get when you cross a few islands in the Pacific and a scary spirit? The *Galapa-ghost* Islands!

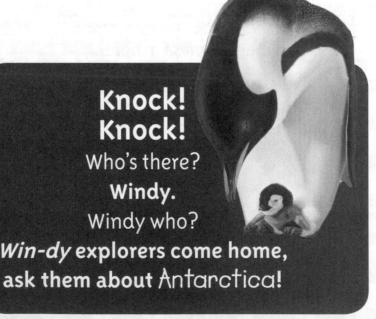

Knock! Knock!
Who's there?
Windy.
Windy who?
Win-dy explorers come home, ask them about Antarctica!

**Knock!
Knock!**
Who's there?
Eel.
Eel who?
Eel **take you to the**
Great Barrier Reef!

**Knock!
Knock!**
Who's there?
Gecko.
Gecko who?
Gecko-ing **or you'll miss
sunset at the** Grand Canyon!

What do you get when you cross
Darwin's idea of natural selection
with an arcade game?
Dance Dance *Evolution*!

What do you get when you cross a Galapagos turtle and a sneeze? A giant *snort*-oise!

Knock! Knock!
Who's there?
Snow.
Snow who?
***Snow*-one knew where Antarctica was until the 1700s!**

Knock! Knock!
Who's there?
Bill.
Bill who?
***Bill*-ieve me when I tell you Niagara Falls is huge!**

Why is the Grand Canyon braver than other national parks?
Because it's so much *boulder*!

Knock! Knock!

Who's there?

Rhonda.

Rhonda who?

Rhon-da **way to** Niagara Falls!

AREAS OF AMERICAN ANTICS

Knock! Knock!
Who's there?
Mickey.
Mickey who?
Mic-key **to my room at** Walt Disney World **is missing!**

Why are Broadway shows so short?
Because they're on Forty-*Seconds* Street!

What do you get when you cross an American river and a person who falls down?
The mighty Missi-*slippy*!

Knock! Knock!
Who's there?
Betty.
Betty who?
Betty or not, we're going to the White House!

Why do cows love Hollywood?
Because of all the *mooovies*!

What did the man say when he used
dynamite to carve Mount Rushmore?
"That was a *blast*!"

Knock!
Knock!
Who's there?
Walleye.
Walleye who?
***Wall-eye* go fishing on the**
Mississippi, **you stay here!**

What part of Walt Disney World do
noses hate to visit?
Cinder-*smell*-a's Castle!

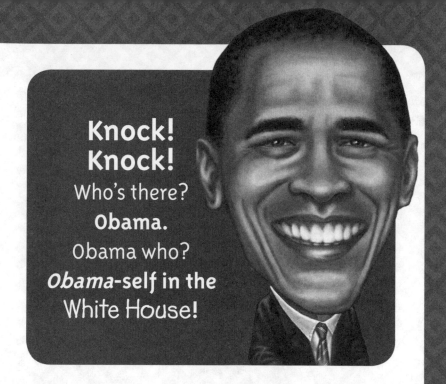

**Knock!
Knock!**
Who's there?
Obama.
Obama who?
Obama-**self in the**
White House!

What do you get when you cross a
Broadway play and a bull rider?
Rodeo and Juliet!

What did the math teacher say
when she moved to Hollywood?
"Lights! Camera! *Fraction!*"

Knock!
Knock!
Who's there?
Annie.
Annie who?
Annie-**body want to see a**
Broadway **musical with me?**

HOLLYWOOD

What do you get when you
cross a famous Hollywood
intersection and a pig?
Hollywood & *swine*!

What part of Walt Disney World
has the most sneezes?
Ep-*snot*!

Knock!
Knock!

Who's there?

Washington.

Washington who?

***Washing-tons* of clothes is easy in the White House laundry room!**

Knock!
Knock!

Who's there?

Theodore.

Theodore who?

***The-odore* of prairie dogs makes Mount Rushmore stinky!**

What do you get when you cross a Broadway play and a fibber? The *Lyin'* King!

Knock! Knock!
Who's there?
Indie.
Indie who?
In-die **film world, many movies are made in** Hollywood**!**

Which Star Wars character loves Walt Disney World? *Or-Lando* Calrissian!

What do you get when you cross a **Broadway** show with a smoothie? *Fruity* and the Beast!

Knock! Knock!
Who's there?
Huckleberry Finn.
Huckleberry Finn who?
Huckleberry, Finn-ish writing that book about the Mississippi!

Why did the sculptor carve so deep into **Mount Rushmore**? Because he was working in the *Great Depression*.

Knock! Knock!

Who's there?

Oscar.

Oscar who?

***Os-car* a question about her** Hollywood **movie!**

What part of
Walt Disney World
do raisins like to visit?

Bran-tasyland!

What floor of the White House
has the best coffee?
The *ground* floor!

Why did the sculptor work fast when he was carving Thomas Jefferson's face?
Because he had to *Rush-more*!

Where do whales like to sit when they see a **Broadway** show?
By the *orca*-stra!

Knock! Knock!
Who's there?
Levee.
Levee who?
Levee **borrow your canoe for my trip down the** Mississippi!

What do you get when you cross a ride at **Walt Disney World** and a deck of cards?
Ace Mountain!

What did the boat say when it entered the **Mississippi River** without asking?
"Sorry to *barge* in on you!"

Where does the president go canoeing at the **White House?**
In the *Rows* Garden!

Why is Christmas so popular in Hollywood?
Because it's *Tinsel*-town!

HOLLYWOOD

**Knock!
Knock!**
Who's there?
Curt.
Curt who?
Curt-ain call in five minutes for a Broadway show!

Why did the dentist go to Walt Disney World?
To see A-*denture*-land!

Why do discussions in the Oval Office take so long?

Because the conversation goes around in *circles*!

Knock! Knock!

Who's there?

Tom Sawyer.

Tom Sawyer who?

Tom, Saw-yer **riverboat heading down the** Mississippi!

What do you get when you cross Mount Rushmore with a baby's diaper?

Mount *Rash*-more!

What do you get when you cross the **White House** visitor center with a dragon?
The *Beast* Wing!

Knock! Knock!
Who's there?
Nemo.
Nemo who?
***Nemo* tickets to Walt Disney World!**

What do you get when you cross **Hollywood** stars and Santa Claus?
The *Jolly*-wood Walk of Fame!

Knock! Knock!

Who's there?

Mrs.

Mrs. who?

Mrs. Sippi **River!**

Knock! Knock!

Who's there?

Howard.

Howard who?

How-ard **I learn more about** Broadway **show tunes?**

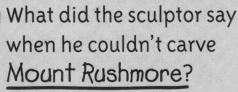

What did the sculptor say when he couldn't carve <u>Mount Rushmore?</u>

"My chisel isn't making a presi-*dent* in this rock!"

Why aren't there any crayons in the **White House?**

Because it's on *Pencil*-vania Avenue!

What does a **Mississippi River** steamboat weigh?

About a *Fulton*!

Knock! Knock!

Who's there?

Ben.

Ben who?

Ben **to Mount Rushmore and I can't wait to go back again!**

Knock! Knock!
Who's there?
Cats.
Cats who?
Cats me in a play on Broadway!

Why did Hollywood do badly in school?
Because it had *3-Ds*!

Knock! Knock!
Who's there?
Donald.
Donald who?
Don-ald the rides there are at Walt Disney World!

Knock! Knock!

Who's there?

Mark Twain.

Mark Twain who?

Mark Twain-d to be a captain on the Mississippi River!

Why did the sculptor of Mount Rushmore have itchy skin?

Because of all the dyna-*mites*!

Which Broadway show likes to eat sandwiches?

Ham-ilton!

Why is the White House
so uncomfortable?
Because everyone is in the *cabinet*!

**Knock!
Knock!**
Who's there?
Mountain.
Mountain who?
Mountain **a horse to ride
to** Mount Rushmore!

What did
Walt Disney World
say when it was
accused of not
playing fair?
"I'd never *resort*
to cheating!"

Knock! Knock!

Who's there?

Justin.

Justin who?

Just-in time for my Broadway show!

Why did the cowboy cry
at Walt Disney World?

Because he was in Fron-*tear*-land!

Why is it so bright in Hollywood?
Because of all the *stars*!

Where does the president
drink his hot chocolate?
In the *Oval-tine* Office!

What do you say to the
Mississippi River when you
want it to stop begging?
"*Down*, river!"

Knock!
Knock!
Who's there?
Hollywood.
Hollywood who?
Holly-wood love to
visit a movie set!

Knock!
Knock!
Who's there?
Olaf.
Olaf who?
O-laf a lot when I'm at
Walt Disney World!

What do you get when you
cross Mount Rushmore
and a parent?
A national *mom*-ument!

Why can't you steal the **Mississippi River?**
Because it has too many *locks*!

**Knock!
Knock!**
Who's there?
Abbey.
Abbey who?
Abbey waiting to see my favorite Broadway musical!

BUILT TO LAUGH

Knock! Knock!
Who's there?
Jewel.
Jewel who?
Jewel **be amazed at all the precious stones in the** Taj Mahal!

Why did the Empire State Building go to the library?
Because it has so many *stories*.

Why does James Bond like the Eiffel Tower?
Because of all the *spy*-ral staircases!

Knock! Knock!

Who's there?

Ferry.

Ferry who?

Ferry **many boats travel under the** Brooklyn Bridge!

Knock! Knock!

Who's there?

Sandee.

Sandee who?

Sand-dee **bars down so we can escape** <u>Alcatraz</u>!

Knock! Knock!

Who's there?

Olive.

Olive who?

***O-live* the <u>Empire State Building</u>!**

What did the prison guard say to the messy prisoner?

"Hey! Clean up your Alca-*trash*!"

Knock! Knock!

Who's there?

India.

India who?

***In-dia* Taj Mahal, there's lots of rooms!**

Knock! Knock!
Who's there?
Sue.
Sue who?
Sue-venir shops sell tiny statues of the Eiffel Tower!

What language does the Brooklyn Bridge like to study?
Span-ish!

What did the guard say to the tourist at the Taj Mahal when he went inside without a ticket?
"Hey, wait a *minaret*!"

Knock! Knock!

Who's there?

Water.

Water who?

Wat-er you waiting for? Let's swim away from Alcatraz Island!

What did the tourist say when he was stuck in traffic on the way to the Taj Mahal?

"This is so *Agra*-vating!"

Knock! Knock!
Who's there?
Iron.
Iron who?
Iron fifty cents an hour building the Eiffel Tower!

Why was the Brooklyn Bridge sent home from school?
It got *suspended*!

Why do the prisoners on Alcatraz have so many pimples?
Because they like to *break out*!

Knock! Knock!

Who's there?

Candice.

Candice who?

Can-dice photo of the Empire State Building be any prettier?

What do you get when you cross the <u>Eiffel Tower</u> and corn?

A *cob*-servation deck!

Who is the Brooklyn Bridge's sister?

Brooklyn *Bridget!*

**Knock!
Knock!**
Who's there?
Mahal.
Mahal who?
Ma-hal **your dreams come true
when you visit the** Taj Mahal**!**

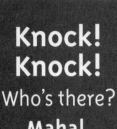

Why did the French
man jump off the
<u>Eiffel Tower</u>?
Because he had a
Paris-chute!

Why don't the inmates of
Alcatraz eat chocolate?
Because they don't like *bars*.

Knock! Knock!

Who's there?

Eiffel.

Eiffel who?

***Eif-fel* in love with the tower the first time I saw it!**

Why did the pig walk across the Brooklyn Bridge?

To get to New *Pork* City!

How do the inmates at Alcatraz make phone calls?

Using their *cell* phones.

What did the magician say when he made the towers near the Taj Mahal disappear?

"*Mausoleum*, now you don't!"

What's the most popular book in Alcatraz?

War-den Peace!

What did the Empire State Building drink when it needed more energy?

Tower-ade!

What did the **Brooklyn Bridge** say when it drank too much coffee? "I'm so totally *wired*!"

What kinds of stories do criminals read on **Alcatraz**? Nursery *crimes*!

Knock! Knock!
Who's there?
Divine.
Divine who?
Di-vines **on the walls of the** Taj Mahal **are so pretty!**

Why was Gustave Eiffel so close with his famous tower?
Because they had a beautiful *French*-ship!

Knock! Knock!
Who's there?
Wanda.
Wanda who?
Wanda **go to the** Empire State Building **with me?**

What do you get when you cross the <u>Brooklyn Bridge</u> and an icebox?
The Brooklyn *Fridge*!

What did the frog say when it saw the Eiffel Tower?

Rivet! Rivet!

Knock! Knock!

Who's there?

Art.

Art who?

Art Deco **buildings like the** Empire State Building **were built in the 1920s and 1930s!**

What do you get when you cross the gardens at the Taj Mahal and a game of billiards?

A reflecting *pool table*!

What musical notes does the <u>Taj Mahal</u> sing?
Dome-re-mi!

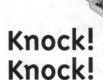

Knock! Knock!
Who's there?
Al.
Al who?
***Al-catraz*, the famous island prison!**

Why don't the Brooklyn Bridge's pants ever fall down?
Because it has so many *suspenders*!

What do you get when you cross the **Empire State Building** and dinner?
The Empire *Steak* Building.

Knock! Knock!
Who's there?
Elle.
Elle who?
***Elle-vators* carry people to the top of the** Eiffel Tower!

Why do people get colds in the **Taj Mahal?**
Because of all the *coffin*!

Why did Al Capone only use pens to write his letters from <u>Alcatraz</u>?
Because it's not a *pencil*-itentiary!

Why did the **Empire State Building** get so famous?
It wanted to a-*spire* to something great!

What did the builder say when someone took the Brooklyn Bridge? "Hey, that's *steel*-ing!"

Why are there no security officers inside the Taj Mahal? Because they're in the *guard*-ens!

Knock! Knock!
Who's there?
Stopwatch.
Stopwatch who?
Stop-watch you're doing! It's time for the Empire State Building lights to come on!

Why does the Brooklyn Bridge watch so much TV?
Because it loves *cable*!

What do you get when you cross Alcatraz with a yummy dessert?
Jail-O pudding!

Why did the Eiffel Tower keep squirming in its chair?
Because it had *France* in its pants!

Why can't the Taj Mahal count to three?
Because it's only a *two*-mb!

Knock! Knock!
Who's there?
Seine.
Seine who?
Seine a lot of towers, but none as pretty as the Eiffel!

What is the Empire State Building's favorite relative?
Its *aunt-tenna*!

What do you get when you cross the <u>Empire State Building</u> and a baseball game? The *Umpire* State Building!

Knock! Knock!
Who's there?
Wire.
Wire who?
***Wire* you taking pictures of the Brooklyn Bridge?**

What do you get when you cross the Eiffel Tower and a lemon? An Eiffel *Sour*!

MYSTERIOUS PLACES OF MISCHIEF

Knock! Knock!
Who's there?
Carrie.
Carrie who?
Carrie-bbean **storms make the** Bermuda Triangle **dangerous!**

What do you get when you cross **Area 51** and a pizza chef?
A flying *saucer*!

What did the Amazon say when it kicked out the poachers?
Don't let the equa-*door* hit you on the way out!

Knock! Knock!
Who's there?
Ahu.
Ahu who?
Ahu **built the statues on** Easter Island?

What do you get when you cross the galaxy with a dentist?
A *molar* system!

Knock! Knock!
Who's there?
Fuels.
Fuels who?
Fuels **dare to trespass**
at Area 51!

Why did Stonehenge
have to stay home
from school?
Because the doctor said it
had swollen En-*glands*!

Why did the scientist like to swim
at Easter Island?
Because she was an anthro-*pool*-ogist!

Knock! Knock!

Who's there?

Peru.

Peru who?

***Peru* going on a trip to the** Amazon**?**

Why did Jupiter's pants fall down?
It wasn't wearing its asteroid *belt*!

Knock! Knock!

Who's there?

Disappear.

Disappear who?

***Dis-appears* to be where the plane crashed in the** Bermuda Triangle**!**

Knock! Knock!
Who's there?
Avenue.
Avenue who?
Aven-ue **heard of the road that leads to** Stonehenge?

What did Easter Island say when its volcano first erupted? "I *lava* you!"

What do animals eat when they barbecue in the Amazon? Hot dogs and cole-*sloth*!

Why did the Bermuda Triangle join a gym?

It wanted to get in *shape*!

Knock! Knock!

Who's there?

Juno.

Juno who?

Ju-no that satellites are taking pictures of Jupiter?

What did the government agent say when he saw a baby flying over Area 51?

"I'd like to report an Unidentified *Crying* Object!"

Knock! Knock!

Who's there?

Chile.

Chile who?

Chile **weather rarely hits** Easter Island**!**

What do you get when you cross the Bermuda Triangle and some nachos?

A *chip*-wreck!

What do you get when you cross the Amazon with the human mind?

A tropical *brain*-forest!

Why did the astronaut miss her landing on the moon?
She didn't *planet* right!

Knock! Knock!
Who's there?
Megalith.
Megalith who?
Meg-a-lith **of all the things you love about** Stonehenge!

Why did the Jedi go to Area 51?
He heard they had a lot of Air *Force*!

Why is the Bermuda Triangle never late?
Because of all the *hurry*-canes!

Knock! Knock!
Who's there?
Phyllis.
Phyllis who?
***Phyll-is* in on everything you saw in the Amazon!**

Which planet likes to play the guitar?
Nep-*tune*!

Why won't the military talk about the spinning toys at Area 51? They're *top* secret!

Why are there so many drawings of Stonehenge? Because of all the *drew*-ids!

Knock! Knock!
Who's there?
Statue.
Statue who?
Stat-ue hiding behind the heads on Easter Island?

Knock! Knock!
Who's there?
Ana.
Ana who?
Ana-condas slither
through the Amazon!

Where do people look for
things that have gone missing
in the Bermuda Triangle?
The lost and *not* found.

Knock! Knock!
Who's there?
Rover.
Rover who?
Rover there is the planet Mars!

Why did the bride go to Area 51?
To visit *Groom* Lake!

Why does Stonehenge
always have a tan?
Because it was built during the
Bronze Age!

Why weren't the sailors hungry
on the way to Easter Island?
Because of Captain *Cook*!

Knock!
Knock!

Who's there?

Juan.

Juan who?

Juan **are you coming to the** Bermuda Triangle?

Why did the space aliens drop off their passenger at Area 51? Because they had an *extra*-terrestrial!

What do you call the chickens who live at Stonehenge? *Stone*-hens!

What do you call the Amazon River
when the water stops flowing?
The Amaz-*off* River!

Knock! Knock!

Who's there?

The Moai.

The Moai who?

***The Mo-ai* see the statues on** Easter
Island, **the more I like them.**

What did Galileo say to himself when he
got excited about the Solar System?
"*Comet* down!"

Knock!
Knock!
Who's there?
Spy.
Spy who?
Spy **wouldn't take pictures of**
<u>Area 51</u> **if I were you!**

What romance website
does Stonehenge use?
Carbon-dating.com!

WARNING
UFO
MILITARY INSTALLATION

IT IS UNLAWFUL TO ENTER THIS INSTALLATION WITHOUT
THE WRITTEN PERMISSION OF THE INSTALLATION COMMANDER

I BELIEVE!

INSTALLATION COMMANDER
AUTHORITY: Internal Security Act, 50
U.S.C. 797
PUNISHMENT: Up to one year imprisonment
and $5,000 fine.

Why did the captain have trouble
finding Easter Island?
His directions weren't *Pacific* enough!

What do people in the Amazon put on their toast?

Butter-flies!

Knock! Knock!
Who's there?
Toucan.
Toucan who?
***Tou-can* fit in my canoe on the Amazon!**

Why are there two of everything in the Bermuda Triangle?
Because of all the cy-*clones*!

Knock! Knock!
Who's there?
Salisbury.
Salisbury who?
Sal's-bury-d **a lot of bones near** Stonehenge!

What did the explorer say to the statues on Easter Island when they got into a fight?
"The bigger they are, the *Heyerdahl* fall!"

How long is the Amazon River?
About a *Brazilian* miles!

**Knock!
Knock!**
Who's there?
Sink.
Sink who?
Sink **twice before you decide to enter the** Bermuda Triangle.

**Knock!
Knock!**
Who's there?
Moon.
Moon who?
Moon **over so I can look
through the telescope!**

What do you get when you cross
Stonehenge and a scoop of ice cream?
Cone-henge!

Why did the space creature at Area 51 read the Declaration of Independence? Because he had certain in-*alien*-able rights!

Why did Saturn get a stomachache? It *orbit* off more than it could chew!

Knock! Knock!
Who's there?
Thor.
Thor who?
Thor <u>Easter Island</u> →
with an experienced guide!

Why is the Bermuda Triangle so scary?
Because it's in the Gulf *Scream*!

**Knock!
Knock!**
Who's there?
Archie.
Archie who?
Archie-ologists discovered the
secrets of Stonehenge!

Where does the Amazon River
keep all its money?
In *river* banks.

Knock! Knock!

Who's there?

Compass.

Compass who?

Com-pass some time with me
in the Bermuda Triangle!

Why are the people of Easter Island so good at making hip-hop music?
Because they're members of the *Rapa* Nui tribe!

What did the soldier say when asked about the location of **Area 51**?
"*Nevada* heard of it!"